# Dinosaur Cousins?

Written
and
illustrated
by
Bernard Most

Harcourt Brace Jovanovich, Publishers
San Diego   New York   London

The illustrations in this book were done in Pantone markers on hot press board.
The text type was set in Avant Garde Gothic Book by Thompson Type, San Diego, California.
The display type was set in Avant Garde Gothic Medium by Thompson Type, San Diego, California.
Printed and bound by South China Printing Co., Hong Kong
Designed by Francesca M. Smith
Production supervision by Warren Wallerstein

Requests for permission to make copies of any part of the work should be mailed to:
Copyrights and Permissions Department, Harcourt Brace Jovanovich, Publishers,
Orlando, Florida 32887.

The author wishes to acknowledge the following books as sources for the factual information contained in the text:
The Day of the Dinosaur by Lyon Sprague De Camp and Catherine Crook
Dinosaurs, An Illustrated History by Edwin R. Colbert
A Field Guide to Dinosaurs by David Lambert
The New Larousse Encyclopedia of Animal Life by Larousse and Co.
World Guide to Mammals by Nicole Duplaix and Noel Simon

Library of Congress Cataloging-in-Publication Data
Most, Bernard.
    Dinosaur cousins?
    Bibliography: p.
    Summary: Examines nineteen modern animals and describes the dinosaurs they resemble in appearance or behavior, making such comparisons as the giraffe to the long-necked brachiosaurus and the armadillo to the armored ankylosaurus.
    1. Dinosaurs—Juvenile literature. 2. Animals—Juvenile literature. [1. Dinosaurs. 2. Animals] I. Title.
QE862.D5M69   1987      567.9'1      86-18485
ISBN 0-15-223497-7
ISBN 0-15-223498-5 (pbk.)

C D E F G
B C D E (pbk.)

*To my father,*
*who taught me much about color*

I know that there are no dinosaurs anymore. But whenever I go to the zoo, or read a book about animals, I see so many animals that remind me of dinosaurs. I wonder . . .

Are they dinosaur cousins?

Is a rhinoceros a dinosaur cousin?
A rhinoceros reminds me of a triceratops.

A triceratops walked on all four legs and had horns like a rhinoceros. Even though it looked dangerous, a triceratops attacked only if it was attacked first—just like our rhinoceros. If the triceratops were alive today, I think the rhinoceros would be its best friend.

Is a duck a dinosaur cousin?
A duck reminds me of a hadrosaurus.

A hadrosaurus was a "duckbilled dinosaur." Webbed fingers and webbed toes, along with a flat tail, made it a very good swimmer. Fossils of footprints suggest that hadrosaurus mothers probably watched out for their young, just like mother ducks do. I wonder if they were able to quack like ducks.

Is a roadrunner a dinosaur cousin?

A roadrunner reminds me of an avimimus.

Avimimus means "bird mimic." Fossils showing real feathered wings and tail prove the avimimus was a feathered dinosaur. Many scientists believe birds are living dinosaur cousins. Like our modern roadrunner, the avimimus ran at fast speed to catch its dinner, instead of flying.

Are porcupines dinosaur cousins?

A porcupine reminds me of a kentrosaurus.

A kentrosaurus, which means "pointed lizard," was like a giant porcupine. Its body was protected by pointed, bony plates and sharp spikes. Like a porcupine, it was a plant-eater and would use its spikes if it was attacked. Do you think meat-eating dinosaurs got the point?

Are kangaroos dinosaur cousins?
A kangaroo reminds me of a kakuru.

Because of very long legs and a very long tail, scientists think kakurus were able to make high leaps, like kangaroos. The name *kakuru* even sounds like kangaroo, and fossils of kakurus were found in Australia, home of the kangaroo. Maybe someday scientists will discover a dinosaur with a pouch.

Is a moose a dinosaur cousin?
A moose reminds me of a lambeosaurus.

A lambeosaurus had a large, bony crest that looked like a moose's antlers. Scientists think it used the crest to make loud, horn-like toots. Moose make a sound like that when they call each other. The lambeosaurus once lived in Canada and the northern United States, homes of the moose today.

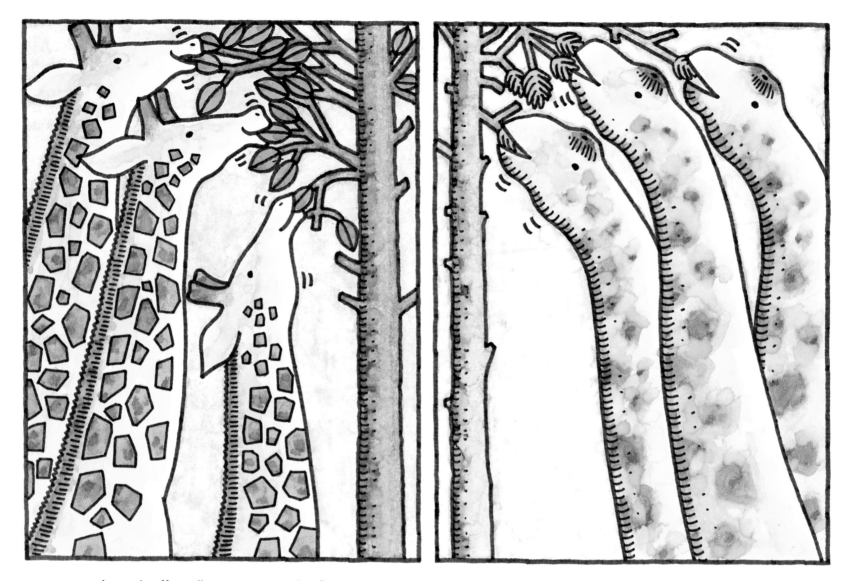

Are giraffes dinosaur cousins?

A giraffe reminds me of a brachiosaurus.

With one of the longest necks of any dinosaur, a brachiosaurus was like a giant giraffe. Like a giraffe, it used its long neck for reaching leaves on the tallest trees. On top of its head, a brachiosaurus had a bony crest. A giraffe has bony horns on top of its head.

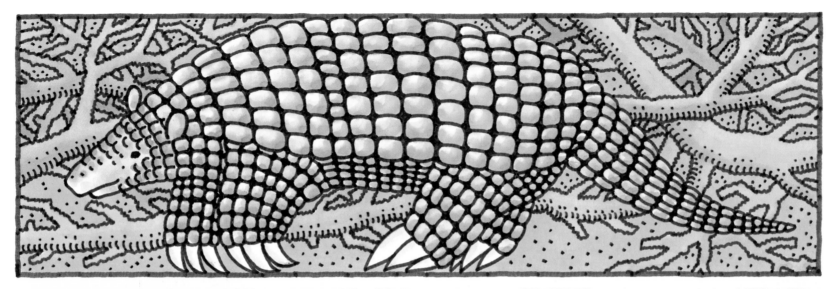

Are armadillos dinosaur cousins?

An armadillo reminds me of an ankylosaurus.

An armadillo gets its protection from rows and rows of bony plates of armor. An ankylosaurus had a low, barrel-shaped body covered by rows of bony plates of armor, which protected it from bigger dinosaurs. Scientists think the ankylosaurus lived on insects. An armadillo's favorite meal is insects.

Are musk oxen dinosaur cousins?
A musk ox reminds me of a styracosaurus.

Musk oxen form a circle whenever they are attacked by wolves. Their sharp horns protect the younger and weaker musk oxen in the center. Patterns of fossils have been found showing that herds of the plant-eating styracosaurus also formed circles for protection from meat-eating dinosaurs.

Is an ostrich a dinosaur cousin?
An ostrich reminds me of a struthiomimus.

Struthiomimus means "ostrich mimic." I can see why it got this name. An ostrich is one of the fastest animals in the world today. The struthiomimus was one of the fastest dinosaurs. I would love to see a race between an ostrich and a struthiomimus. I wonder who would win.

Are elephants dinosaur cousins?
An elephant reminds me of a brontosaurus.

Fossils show that brontosaurus ran in herds the same way elephants do. Brontosaurus means "thunder lizard"—it made the ground shake when it walked, just like the ground shakes when a herd of elephants walks through the jungle. I wonder if a brontosaurus liked peanuts.

Are bighorn sheep dinosaur cousins?
Bighorn sheep remind me of stegoceras.

Just like male bighorn sheep, male stegoceras had butting contests with their bony heads, and the winner became leader of the herd. These dinosaurs made their home in the highest hills and mountains, where bighorn sheep live today.

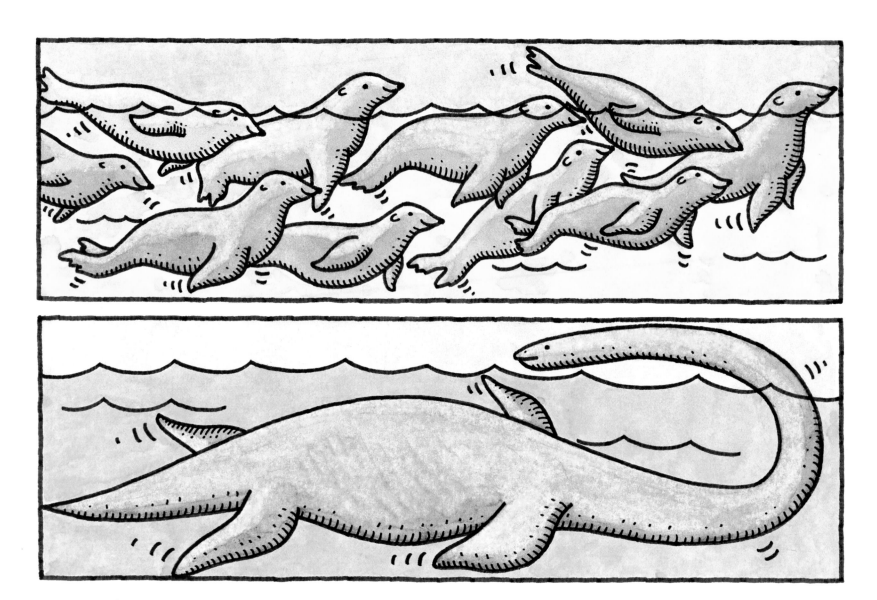

Are seals dinosaur cousins?

A seal reminds me of a plesiosaurus.

A plesiosaurus was actually a close cousin of the dinosaurs. Because of its flippers, a plesiosaurus was a very good swimmer, and it could also breathe out of water, just like a seal. I wonder if a plesiosaurus could have balanced a ball on top of its nose.

Is a gazelle a dinosaur cousin?

A gazelle reminds me of a parasaurolophus.

Today, gazelles roam the plains grazing on grass. The plant-eating dinosaur parasaurolophus was also a grazer, feeding on low plants. When it was in danger, a parasaurolophus could run as fast as a gazelle. Doesn't its curved, hollow horn remind you of a gazelle's antlers?

Is a pelican a dinosaur cousin?
Pelicans remind me of pteranodons.

A pteranodon was a flying cousin of the dinosaurs. It made its home on seaside cliffs, as pelicans do today. Swooping down, it would scoop up fish in its pelican-like beak. It also used its beak to store and carry food back home to its nest.

Are baby chicks dinosaur cousins?

Baby chicks remind me of baby protoceratops.

Nests containing eggs of baby protoceratops have been discovered. Mother protoceratops protected their eggs much like mother hens do today. Many nests were grouped close together, which means the dinosaurs probably took turns helping each other—sort of like a dinosaur nursery.

For me, the dinosaurs are not gone. There are just so many animals living today that remind me of dinosaurs. I'm not a scientist, but it's fun to wonder:
    Are they dinosaur cousins?

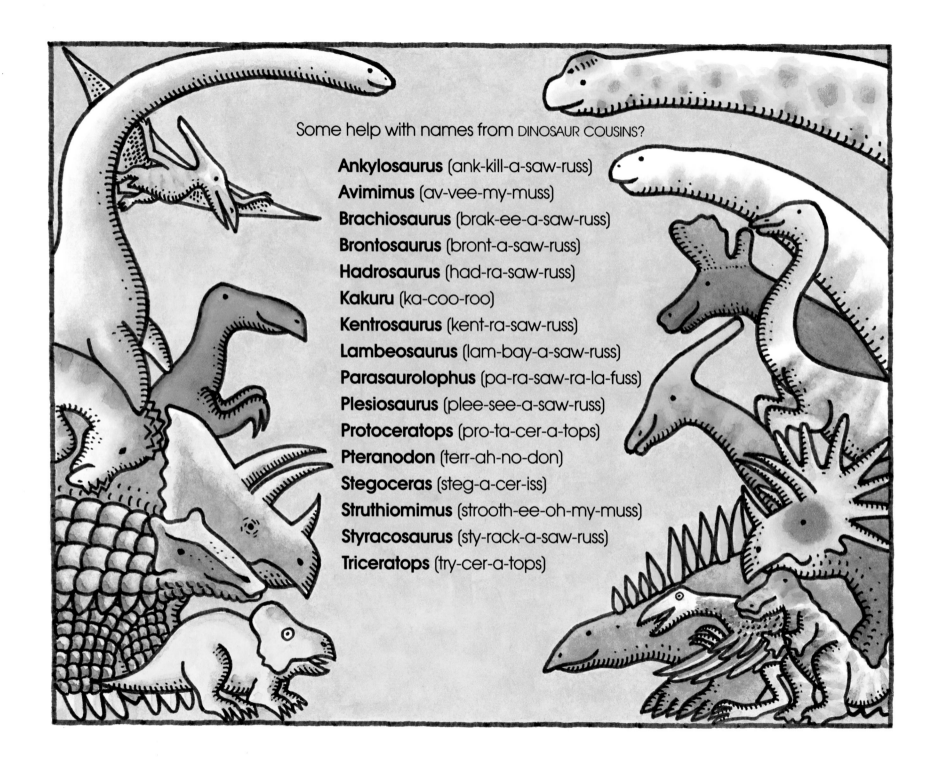

Some help with names from DINOSAUR COUSINS?

**Ankylosaurus** (ank-kill-a-saw-russ)
**Avimimus** (av-vee-my-muss)
**Brachiosaurus** (brak-ee-a-saw-russ)
**Brontosaurus** (bront-a-saw-russ)
**Hadrosaurus** (had-ra-saw-russ)
**Kakuru** (ka-coo-roo)
**Kentrosaurus** (kent-ra-saw-russ)
**Lambeosaurus** (lam-bay-a-saw-russ)
**Parasaurolophus** (pa-ra-saw-ra-la-fuss)
**Plesiosaurus** (plee-see-a-saw-russ)
**Protoceratops** (pro-ta-cer-a-tops)
**Pteranodon** (terr-ah-no-don)
**Stegoceras** (steg-a-cer-iss)
**Struthiomimus** (strooth-ee-oh-my-muss)
**Styracosaurus** (sty-rack-a-saw-russ)
**Triceratops** (try-cer-a-tops)